"This is a good spot for the tent," said Fluffy.

"Yes, we are right across from the beach!" said Charlie.
"Let's go and play in the sand!"

Fluffy said, "I will sit here in the sun. Don't eat the sand Charlie."

Charlie had a lot of fun playing in the sand.
He made this sand castle!

"It's time to get ready for bed," said Fluffy.
"Let's read our books before it gets too dark."

"Okay," said Charlie.
"I will read to you.
Then you can read to me!"

It was getting dark!

"Charlie, come and look at this!" said Fluffy. "The sun is going down!"

Charlie came to have a look.
"The sunset is so beautiful," he said.

That night, Fluffy made a fire.

"Here are some marshmallows for us to eat," said Fluffy.

"I don't like this fire!" said Charlie. "We are too furry to sit by a fire."

He went to bed without eating his marshmallow!

In the morning, Charlie was hungry.
He went to look for something to eat.

Fluffy said, "Look over there.
I see something over there."

Fluffy and Charlie walked over to the snack shack.

At the top of the menu it said, **"Burgers & Dogs"**.

"Burgers and **dogs**!" shouted Charlie.

Charlie ran away as fast as he could.
"Wait for me!" shouted Fluffy.

And they ran all the way home!